Painless Fast Metabolism Diet Recipes For Lazy People

50 Surprisingly Simple Fast Metabolism Diet Cookbook Recipes Even Your Lazy Ass Can Cook

By: Philip Pablo

Painless Fast Metabolism Diet Recipes for Lazy People

TABLE OF CONTENTS

Publishers Notes

Dedication

Introduction to Anti-Inflammatory Diet

A. Recipes by category type

phase 1 breakfast recipes

Meal 1- Lemony Green Smoothie

Meal 2- Chocolaty Quinoa with Raspberries

phase 1 lunch recipes

MEAL 3- Chicken & Black Bean Salad

MEAL 4- Cantaloupe & Lime Soup

MEAL 5- Glazed Chicken with Squash

MEAL 6- Sautéed Cabbage

MEAL 7- Baked Fish & Vegetables with Noodles

phase 1 dinner recipes

MEAL 8- Roasted Vegetable Soup

MEAL 9- Spiced Pork Tenderloin

MEAL 10- White Bean Chicken Chili

Philip Pablo

phase 1 snacks recipes

MEAL 11- Baked Turkey Patties

MEAL 12- Fresh Fruit Salad

phase 1 dessert recipes

MEAL 13- Fresh Strawberry Granita

MEAL 14- Brown Rice Pudding

phase 2 breakfast recipes

MEAL 15- Salmon & Spinach Frittata

MEAL 16- Bacon & Vegetable Muffins

phase 2 lunch recipes

MEAL 17- Green Garden Salad

MEAL 18- Mushroom & Spinach Soup

MEAL 19- Pan Fried Chicken Breasts

MEAL 20- Broiled Beef with Broccoli

Painless Fast Metabolism Diet Recipes for Lazy People

phase 2 dinner recipes

MEAL 21- Beef & Veggie Salad

MEAL 22-Hot Beef & Cabbage Soup

MEAL 23- Roasted Lamb Leg with Rosemary

MEAL 24- Baked Lemony Fish

phase 2 snacks recipes

MEAL 25- Baked Meatballs with Vegetables

MEAL 26- Chicken & Bell Pepper Wraps

phase 2 desserts recipes

MEAL 27- Citrus Sorbet

MEAL 28- Green Popsicles

phase 3 breakfast recipes

MEAL 29- Bacon & Vegetable Frittata

MEAL 30- Bread with Hazelnut Butter and Berries

MEAL 31- Lemony Blueberry Pancakes

MEAL 32- Oats with Almond Butter & Cherries

Philip Pablo

phase 3 lunch recipes

MEAL 33- Pasta & Veggie Salad with Creamy Dressing

MEAL 34- Veggie soup with Quinoa

MEAL 35- Baked Rosemary Chicken & Tomatoes

MEAL 36- Shrimp with Mushrooms

MEAL 37- Grilled Tangy Vegetables

phase 3 lunch recipes

MEAL 38- Spiced Chickpeas & Sweet Potato Salad

MEAL 39- Chicken, Barley & Veggie Soup

MEAL 40- Beef & Green Chiles Stew

MEAL 41- Grilled Lamb Chops with Tomato Salad

MEAL 42- Beans & Vegetables Bake

phase 3 dinner recipes

MEAL 43- Spicy Sweet Potato Wedges

MEAL 44- Herbed Chickpea Patties

MEAL 45- Tangy Cabbage Coleslaw

phase 3 desserts recipes

Painless Fast Metabolism Diet Recipes for Lazy People

MEAL 46- Nutty Oatmeal Cookies

MEAL 47- Grilled Peaches with Glaze

MEAL 48- Rhubarb Compote

MEAL 49- Blackberry Cobble

MEAL 50- Avocado &Mint Mousse

Category by food type

Smoothies

Meal 1- Lemony Green Smoothie

Bread

MEAL 30- Bread with Hazelnut Butter and Berries

Nuts

MEAL 30- Bread with Hazelnut Butter and Berries

MEAL 32- Oats with Almond Butter & Cherries

MEAL 46- Nutty Oatmeal Cookies

Oat

Philip Pablo

MEAL 32- Oats with Almond Butter & Cherries

MEAL 46- Nutty Oatmeal Cookies

Fruits

Meal 2- Chocolaty Quinoa with Raspberries

MEAL 12- Fresh Fruit Salad

MEAL 13- Fresh Strawberry Granita

MEAL 47- Grilled Peaches with Glaze

MEAL 48- Rhubarb Compote

MEAL 49- Blackberry Cobble

MEAL 50- Avocado &Mint Mousse

Rice

MEAL 14- Brown Rice Pudding

Chicken

MEAL 3- Chicken & Black Bean Salad

MEAL 5- Glazed Chicken with Squash

MEAL 10- White Bean Chicken Chili

MEAL 19- Pan Fried Chicken Breasts

Painless Fast Metabolism Diet Recipes for Lazy People

MEAL 26- Chicken & Bell Pepper Wraps

MEAL 35- Baked Rosemary Chicken & Tomatoes

MEAL 39- Chicken, Barley & Veggie Soup

Shrimp

MEAL 36- Shrimp with Mushrooms

Beef

MEAL 20- Broiled Beef with Broccoli

MEAL 21- Beef & Veggie Salad

MEAL 22-Hot Beef & Cabbage Soup

MEAL 25- Baked Meatballs with Vegetables

MEAL 29- Bacon & Vegetable Frittata

MEAL 40- Beef & Green Chiles Stew

Veggies

MEAL 6- Sautéed Cabbage

MEAL 7- Baked Fish & Vegetables with Noodles

MEAL 15- Salmon & Spinach Frittata

MEAL 16- Bacon & Vegetable Muffins

MEAL 21- Beef & Veggie Salad

Philip Pablo

MEAL 25- Baked Meatballs with Vegetables

MEAL 29- Bacon & Vegetable Frittata

MEAL 33- Pasta & Veggie Salad with Creamy Dressing

MEAL 35- Baked Rosemary Chicken & Tomatoes

MEAL 37- Grilled Tangy Vegetables

MEAL 38- Spiced Chickpeas & Sweet Potato Salad

MEAL 42- Beans & Vegetables Bake

MEAL 44- Herbed Chickpea Patties

MEAL 45- Tangy Cabbage Coleslaw

Potato

MEAL 43- Spicy Sweet Potato Wedges

Pasta

MEAL 33- Pasta & Veggie Salad with Creamy Dressing

Fish

MEAL 7- Baked Fish & Vegetables with Noodles

MEAL 15- Salmon & Spinach Frittata

MEAL 17- Green Garden Salad

MEAL 24- Baked Lemony Fish

Painless Fast Metabolism Diet Recipes for Lazy People

Lamb

MEAL 23- Roasted Lamb Leg with Rosemary

MEAL 41- Grilled Lamb Chops with Tomato Salad

Noodles

MEAL 7- Baked Fish & Vegetables with Noodles

Turkey

MEAL 11- Baked Turkey Patties

Soup

MEAL 4- Cantaloupe & Lime Soup

MEAL 8- Roasted Vegetable Soup

MEAL 18- Mushroom & Spinach Soup

MEAL 22-Hot Beef & Cabbage Soup

MEAL 34- Veggie soup with Quinoa

MEAL 39- Chicken, Barley & Veggie Soup

Mushroom

Philip Pablo

MEAL 18- Mushroom & Spinach Soup

Pork

MEAL 9- Spiced Pork Tenderloin

MEAL 16- Bacon & Vegetable Muffins

Books by Phillip Pablo

Recommended Readings

About The Author

Painless Fast Metabolism Diet Recipes for Lazy People

PUBLISHERS NOTES
Disclaimer

This publication is intended to provide helpful and informative material. It is not intended to diagnose, treat, cure, or prevent any health problem or condition, nor is intended to replace the advice of a physician. No action should be taken solely on the contents of this book. Always consult your physician or qualified health-care professional on any matters regarding your health and before adopting any suggestions in this book or drawing inferences from it.

The author and publisher specifically disclaim all responsibility for any liability, loss or risk, personal or otherwise, which is incurred as a consequence, directly or indirectly, from the use or application of any contents of this book.

Any and all product names referenced within this book are the trademarks of their respective owners. None of these owners have sponsored, authorized, endorsed, or approved this book.

Always read all information provided by the manufacturers' product labels before using their products. The author and publisher are not responsible for claims made by manufacturers.

Paperback Edition

Manufactured in the United States of America

Philip Pablo

DEDICATION

This book is dedicated to my mom, who cooks me delicious dinner every day.

Introduction to Fast Metabolism Diet

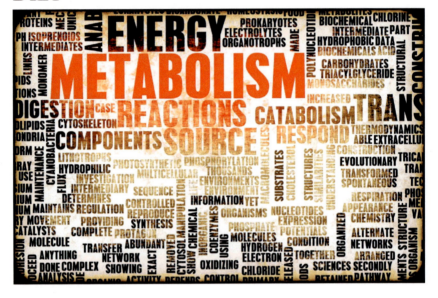

What is fast metabolism diet?

If you have done low-calorie diets and abandon it later, you will understand the limitatione of this diet. You are always starving and this makes your body conserve fats. Unknown to you, you are also not taking in food are causing inflammation. This is slowing your bowels movement and at the same time causing insulin resistance.

In anti-inflammatory diet, there are three phases to use your body's food burning capabilities. You are expected to eat a lot more than other diets. It is recommended that you eat 3 full meals (breakfast, lunch and dinner) and a minimum of 2 snacks everyday. There is no calories counting or avoiding any food groups.

Philip Pablo

The idea is to have different varieties of foods to keep your body burning foods at different speed.

In phase 1, it is designed for Monday and Tuesday. You will eat a lot of fruits and carbs.

In phase 2, it is designed for Weds and Thursday and you will take in a lot of proteins and vegetables.

Lastly, in phase 3, it is for Friday to Sunday and you will take in a lot of foods in phase 1 and 2 and oils plus fats.

At the end of 4 weeks, you will notice that you have lose some weights, your energy level has skyrocketed, you sleep better and you have less stress.

This list of foods is meant to be a rough guide. For complete food lists allowed and disallowed, please refer to "The Fast Metabolism Diet" by Haylie Pomroy.

Food encouraged under fast metabolism diet:
1) Vegetables
2) Fruits
3) Animal proteins
4) Legumes
5) Herbs and spices
6) Natural sweeteners
7) Grains
8) Beverages

Painless Fast Metabolism Diet Recipes for Lazy People

Foods disallowed under fast metabolism diet:
General for 3 phases
1) Wheat
2) Corns
3) Dairy
4) Soy
5) Sugar
6) Caffeine
7) Alchohol
8) Artificiakl sweeteners
9) Fat free foods

Phase 1:
1) Foods in the general list
2) High sugary drinks
3) All fats type
4) Avacado and olives
5) Nuts

Phase 2:
1) Foods in the general list
2) Starchy vegetables
3) Fruits
4) Herbs and spices
5) Fats
6) Avacado and olives
7) Fats

Phase 3:
1) Foods in the general lis
2) Limited carbs
3) Roasted nuts
4) Peanuts

Philip Pablo

phase 1 breakfast recipes

Painless Fast Metabolism Diet Recipes for Lazy People

MEAL 1- LEMONY GREEN SMOOTHIE

Introduction

One of the best and refreshing smoothie recipes. Kick off your day with this refreshing and healthy smoothie.

Preparation Time: 15 minutes

Serves: 2

Ingredients

1. 1 cup spinach, trimmed and torn

2. 1 kiwi, peeled and sliced

3. 1 green apple, peeled, cored and sliced

Philip Pablo

4. 1 cup plain rice milk

5. ½ tablespoon fresh lemon juice

6. 10 drops liquid stevia

7. 1 teaspoon ground cinnamon

8. 4 ice cubes

Preparation of Lemony Green Smoothie

1. In a blender, add all ingredients and pulse till smooth.

2. Pour into glasses and serve immediately.

Calorie Count: Calories are 128 per serving

MEAL 2- CHOCOLATY QUINOA WITH RASPBERRIES

Philip Pablo

Introduction

A great way to start off your day. This chocolaty quinoa recipe is ideal for a delicious breakfast.

Preparation Time: 5 minutes

Cooking Time: 15 minutes

Serves: 1

Ingredients

1. ¼ cup quinoa

2. ½ cup plain rice milk

3. 1/8 teaspoon raw cacao powder

4. Pinch of ground cinnamon

5. 1 cup fresh raspberries

Preparation of Chocolaty Quinoa with Raspberries

1. In a pan, add quinoa and rice milk and bring to a boil on medium heat.

2. Reduce the heat to low. Cover and simmer for about 15 minutes.

3. Turn off the heat. Keep the pan covered for at least 5 minutes.

4. Stir in cacao powder and cinnamon.

5. Transfer the quinoa into a serving plate. Garnish with berries and serve.

Painless Fast Metabolism Diet Recipes for Lazy People

Calorie Count: Calories are 277 per serving

Philip Pablo

phase 1 lunch recipes

MEAL 3- CHICKEN & BLACK BEAN SALAD

Philip Pablo

Introduction

This healthy salad is so colorful, and your family will love eating it. It is filled with the right balance of meat, beans, and vegetables.

Preparation Time: 15 minutes

Serves: 4

Ingredients

1. 1 cup broiled chicken, cut into bite size pieces
2. 1/3 cup cooked black beans
3. ½ cup tomatoes, chopped
4. ½ cup red onion, chopped
5. ¼ cup scallions, chopped
6. 2 cups lettuce, torn
7. Sea salt and freshly ground black pepper, to taste

Preparation of Chicken & Black Beans Salad

1. In a large serving bowl, add all ingredients and mix.
2. Season with salt and black pepper and serve.

Calorie Count: Calories are 123 per serving

MEAL 4- CANTALOUPE & LIME SOUP

Introduction

A super quick chilled soup recipe. This refreshing soup is a great way to dress up your lunch or dinner.

Preparation Time: 10 minutes

Serves: 4

Ingredients

1. 4 cups cantaloupe, peeled, seeded and chopped

2. 3 tablespoons freshly squeezed lime juice

3. ½ cup plus 1 tablespoon fresh mint leaves, divided

4. Sea salt and freshly ground black pepper, to taste

Philip Pablo

Preparation of Cantaloupe & Lime Soup

1. Add all ingredients in a large blender and pulse till smooth.

2. Transfer into a bowl. Cover and refrigerate to chill for about 1 to 1½ hours.

3. Garnish with remaining mint leaves before serving.

Calorie Count: Calories are 61 per serving

Painless Fast Metabolism Diet Recipes for Lazy People

MEAL 5- GLAZED CHICKEN WITH SQUASH

Introduction

A super simple and delicious mustard and balsamic vinegar glazed chicken with butternut squash. This glaze is the perfect complement for chicken.

Preparation Time: 15 minutes

Cooking Time: 30 minutes

Serves: 4

Ingredients

1. 4 (4-ounce) skinless, boneless organic chicken breasts

2. Sea salt and black pepper, to taste

3. 1½ pounds butternut squash, peeled, seeded and cubed

4. 2 tablespoons fresh rosemary, chopped

5. 2 teaspoons balsamic vinegar

For Glaze

1. 1 garlic clove, minced

2. 2 teaspoons fresh ginger, minced

3. 3 teaspoons sugar-free Dijon mustard

4. 2 teaspoons balsamic vinegar

Preparation of Glazed Chicken with Squash

1. Preheat the oven to 400 degrees F. Place the rack in lower third of oven. Line a roasting pan with parchment paper.

2. Arrange chicken breasts on prepared roasting pan. Sprinkle with salt and black pepper evenly.

3. Arrange squash around chicken breasts. Sprinkle squash with a little salt and black pepper.

4. Now, sprinkle chicken and squash with rosemary evenly. Drizzle with vinegar.

5. Bake for about 15 minutes.

Painless Fast Metabolism Diet Recipes for Lazy People

6. Meanwhile in a bowl, add all glaze ingredients and mix till well combined.

7. Flip the chicken breasts over, and coat with glaze generously.

8. Flip the squash over and bake with chicken for 15 minutes more.

Calorie Count: Calories are 206 per serving

Philip Pablo

MEAL 6- SAUTÉED CABBAGE

Painless Fast Metabolism Diet Recipes for Lazy People

Introduction

Enjoy this easy and tasty dish, the delicate flavor of cabbage shines through in this super quick and simple recipe.

Preparation Time: 10 minutes

Cooking Time: 10 minutes

Serves: 2

Ingredients

1. 6 tablespoons homemade chicken broth
2. ½ small onion, chopped finely
3. 1 garlic clove, chopped
4. 1 pound cabbage, chopped
5. ¼ teaspoon coconut aminos
6. Sea salt and black pepper, to taste

Preparation of Sautéed Cabbage

1. In a non-stick skillet, heat broth on medium heat.
2. Add onion and sauté for 3 to 4 minutes.
3. Add garlic and sauté for 1 minute.
4. Add cabbage and sauté for about 4 to 5 minutes.

5. Stir in coconut aminos, salt and black pepper, and cook for 1 to 2 minutes.

6. Remove from heat and serve immediately.

Calorie Count: Calories are 74 per serving

MEAL 7- BAKED FISH & VEGETABLES WITH NOODLES

Introduction

This quick and easy fish recipe is ideal for the busiest weekdays. Cooking the fish and veggies in aluminum foil keeps the fish amazingly moist.

Preparation Time: 15 minutes

Cooking Time: 15 minutes

Serves: 4

Philip Pablo

Ingredients

1. 1 jalapeño, seeded and minced
2. 1 tablespoon fresh ginger, minced
3. ¼ cup fresh lime juice
4. ¼ cup tamari
5. 4 (6-ounce) skinless, boneless haddock fillets
6. 1 cup green bell pepper, seeded and sliced thinly
7. ½ cup fresh mushrooms, sliced thinly
8. 1 cup snap peas
9. ½ cup cabbage, shredded
10. ¼ cup scallions, sliced into thin strips
11. 1 cup buckwheat noodles

Preparation of Baked Fish & Vegetables with Noodles

1. Preheat the oven to 425 degrees F.

2. In a bowl, add jalapeño, ginger, lime juice and tamari, and mix till well combined.

3. Add fish fillets and coat generously. Put aside for 10 minutes.

4. In a bowl, mix together all vegetables.

5. Place 4 heavy-duty aluminum foil sheets on a smooth surface.

6. Divide vegetable mixture evenly on the aluminum sheets.

7. Now, arrange fish fillets on top of vegetables.

8. Drizzle with remaining ginger mixture.

9. Fold the foil to seal the packets of fish and vegetables.

10. Bake for about 13 to 15 minutes.

11. Meanwhile in a pan of boiling water, add noodles and cook for 8 to 10 minutes.

12. Drain and rinse the noodles.

13. On 4 serving plates, divide noodles evenly. Top with fish and vegetable mixture and serve hot.

Calorie Count: Calories are 317 per serving

Philip Pablo

phase 1 dinner recipes

MEAL 8- ROASTED VEGETABLE SOUP

Introduction

This hearty soup is really lovely served for lunch on a cold day. It has a wonderful flavor because of the roasted vegetables.

Preparation Time: 15 minutes

Cooking Time: 40 minutes

Serves: 4

Ingredients

1. 1 medium orange sweet potato, peeled and chopped

2. 5 large carrots, peeled and chopped

3. 1 onion, cut into 8 wedges

4. 4 garlic cloves, peeled

5. 2 tablespoons fresh lemon juice

6. 1 tablespoon lemon zest, freshly grated

7. Sea salt and freshly ground black pepper, to taste

8. 4 cups homemade chicken broth

9. 2 tablespoons fresh cilantro leaves

Preparation of Roasted Vegetable Soup

1. Preheat the oven to 400 degrees F. Line a roasting pan with aluminum foil.

2. In a large bowl, add all ingredients except broth and scallions, and toss to coat well.

3. Transfer the vegetable mixture onto prepared roasting pan.

4. Roast for about 30 to 35 minutes, flipping after every 10 minutes. Remove from oven and cool slightly.

5. In a blender, add vegetables and broth and pulse till smooth.

6. Transfer the puréed soup into a large pan on medium heat.

7. Cook for about 4 to 5 minutes or till heated completely.

8. Garnish with scallions and serve hot.

Painless Fast Metabolism Diet Recipes for Lazy People

Calorie Count: Calories are 120 per serving

Philip Pablo

MEAL 9- S̶piced P̶ork T̶enderloin

Introduction

A great recipe to serve to a hungry crowd . This mixture of herbs and spice rub adds a wonderful twist to grilled pork.

Preparation Time: 10 minutes

Cooking Time: 20 minutes

Serves: 8

Ingredients

1. 2 teaspoons mixed dried herbs (thyme, oregano, rosemary), crushed

2. ½ teaspoon chili powder

Painless Fast Metabolism Diet Recipes for Lazy People

3. ½ teaspoon red pepper flakes, crushed

4. ½ teaspoon ground cumin

5. 1 teaspoon onion powder

6. Sea salt and freshly ground black pepper, to taste

7. 2 (1 pound) pork tenderloins

Preparation of Spiced Pork Tenderloin

1. Preheat the grill to indirect heat.

2. In a large bowl, add herbs and spices and mix well.

3. Add pork tenderloins and coat with spice mixture generously. Put aside for 10 minutes.

4. Place the pork on grill grate. Cover and cook for about 20 minutes, flipping once after 10 minutes.

Calorie Count: Calories are 231 per serving

Philip Pablo

MEAL 10- WHITE BEAN CHICKEN CHILI

Introduction

This white chicken chili recipe makes a delicious and hearty meal filled with the flavors of chicken, white beans and spices.

Preparation Time: 10 minutes

Cooking Time: 20 minutes

Serves: 6

Ingredients

1. 4 cups homemade chicken broth

Painless Fast Metabolism Diet Recipes for Lazy People

2. 4 (4-ounce) skinless, boneless organic chicken thighs

3. 1 (15-ounce) can white beans, undrained

4. 1 medium onion, chopped

5. 1 garlic clove, minced

6. 1 (4-ounce) can diced green chiles, undrained

7. 1 teaspoon dried oregano, crushed

8. 1 teaspoon ground cumin

9. ½ teaspoon chili powder

10. Sea salt and ground white pepper, to taste

11. 2 tablespoons fresh cilantro leaves

Preparation of White Bean Chicken Chili

1. In a large soup pan, on medium-high heat, add broth and chicken. Bring to a boil.

2. Reduce the heat to medium-low. Cover and cook for about 15 minutes or till chicken becomes tender.

3. Transfer the chicken onto a plate. Now, cut chicken into bite size pieces.

4. Add chicken and remaining ingredients except cilantro into the pan of broth.

5. Bring to a boil on medium heat. Reduce the heat to low. Cover and simmer for about 5 minutes.

Philip Pablo

6. Garnish with cilantro and serve hot.

Calorie Count: Calories are 374 per serving

Painless Fast Metabolism Diet Recipes for Lazy People

phase 1 snacks recipes

Philip Pablo

MEAL 11- BAKED TURKEY PATTIES

Introduction

These classic turkey patties are mouth watering and delicious.

Preparation Time: 15 minutes

Cooking Time: 30 minutes

Serves: 6

Ingredients

1. 1½ pounds lean ground turkey

2. ¼ cup fresh scallion leaves, chopped

3. 1 garlic clove, minced finely

4. 1 large egg white

5. Sea salt and black pepper, to taste

Preparation of Baked Turkey Patties

1. Preheat the oven to 350 degrees F. Line a baking sheet with parchment paper.

2. Add all ingredients in a large bowl. Mix till well combined.

3. Make 6 patties from mixture.

4. Arrange patties on lined baking sheet in a single layer.

5. Place the baking sheet in oven and bake for about 30 minutes.

Calorie Count: Calories are 167 per serving

Philip Pablo

MEAL 12- FRESH FRUIT SALAD

Introduction

A delectable salad with fresh fruit. This fresh and yummy salad is perfect for a family gathering.

Preparation Time: 20 minutes

Serves: 8

Ingredients

1. 2 tablespoons fresh mint leaves, minced

2. 2 tablespoons fresh lime juice

Painless Fast Metabolism Diet Recipes for Lazy People

3. 1 tablespoon lime zest, freshly grated

4. Pinch of sea salt

5. 2 cups fresh strawberries, hulled and sliced

6. 1 cup fresh blueberries

7. 1 cup fresh raspberries

8. 4 peaches, pitted and sliced

9. 2 kiwi fruit, peeled and sliced

10. 2 tablespoons fresh mint leaves

Preparation of Fresh Fruit Salad

1. In another small bowl, mix together minced mint leaves, lime juice, zest and salt.

2. In a large serving bowl, add all the fruit and mix.

3. Add lime mixture and toss to coat well

4. Top with mint leaves and serve.

Calorie Count: Calories are 64 per serving

Philip Pablo

phase 1 desserts recipes

Painless Fast Metabolism Diet Recipes for Lazy People

MEAL 13- FRESH STRAWBERRY GRANITA

Introduction

A wonderful use for in- season fresh strawberries… This recipe turns the fresh strawberries into a yummy frozen dessert.

Preparation Time: 10 minutes

Serves: 3

Ingredients

1. ½ cup warm water

2. ½ cup xylitol

3. 2 tablespoons fresh lemon juice

4. 3 cups fresh strawberries, hulled and sliced

5. 1 tablespoon fresh mint leaves

Preparation of Fresh Strawberry Granita

1. In a blender, add water and xylitol and pulse till xylitol dissolves completely.

2. Add lemon juice and strawberries and pulse till smooth.

3. Transfer the mixture into a bowl. Cover and freeze for at least 3 hours.

4. Remove from freezer and with a wooden spoon, stir well.

5. Cover and freeze for at least overnight.

6. Remove from freezer and keep aside at room temperature for at least 10 minutes.

7. With a fork, mix the Granita till it becomes fluffy.

8. Garnish with mint leaves and serve.

Calorie Count: Calories are 140 per serving

Painless Fast Metabolism Diet Recipes for Lazy People

MEAL 14- BROWN RICE PUDDING

Introduction

A wonderful twist on a traditional rice pudding…This recipe makes a comforting and healthy, but delicious dessert.

Preparation Time: 10 minutes

Cooking Time: 45 minutes

Serves: 6

Ingredients

1. 4½ cups plain rice milk

Philip Pablo

2. 1 cup brown rice

3. Pinch of sea salt

4. 1 teaspoon liquid stevia

5. 2 teaspoons ground cinnamon, divided

6. 1 teaspoon vanilla extract

Preparation of Brown Rice Pudding

1. In a large pan, add milk, rice and salt and bring to a boil on medium-high heat.

2. Reduce the heat to low. Cover and simmer for about 45 minutes.

3. Remove from heat but keep aside, covered for at least 10 minutes.

4. Sir in stevia, 1 teaspoon of cinnamon and vanilla.

5. Transfer the pudding into serving bowl. Cover and refrigerate to chill before serving.

6. Sprinkle with remaining cinnamon and serve.

Calorie Count: Calories are 194 per serving

phase 2 breakfast recipes

Philip Pablo

MEAL 15- S<small>ALMON</small> & S<small>PINACH</small> F<small>RITTATA</small>

Introduction

A delicious and healthy breakfast or brunch recipe for the whole family. Smoked salmon and fresh basil add delicious flavors to this quick frittata.

Preparation Time: 10 minutes

Cooking Time: 10 minutes

Serves: 2

Painless Fast Metabolism Diet Recipes for Lazy People

Ingredients

1. 1 tablespoon homemade chicken broth

2. 1 small onion, chopped

3. 6 egg whites

4. Pinch of sea salt and black pepper

5. 2-ounces smoked salmon, chopped

6. 1 teaspoon lemon rind, freshly grated

7. 1 cup baby spinach, chopped

8. 1 tablespoon fresh basil, chopped

Preparation of Salmon & Spinach Frittata

1. Preheat the broiler to low heat.

2. In an oven proof skillet, heat broth on medium heat.

3. Add onion and sauté for 4 to 5 minutes.

4. Meanwhile in a bowl, add egg whites, salt and black pepper and beat well.

5. Stir in remaining ingredients. Pour salmon mixture over onion.

6. Now transfer the skillet to the oven. Broil for 5 minutes.

Calorie Count: Calories are 102 per serving

Philip Pablo

MEAL 16- BACON & VEGETABLE MUFFINS

Painless Fast Metabolism Diet Recipes for Lazy People

Introduction

A great and healthy way to get your toddlers to eat healthy vegetables... Bacon and vegetables with egg whites are a perfect combination for these delicious breakfast muffins.

Preparation Time: 20 minutes

Cooking Time: 25 minutes

Serves: 4

Ingredients

1. 2-ounces nitrate-free turkey bacon, chopped
2. 1 cup fresh mushrooms, chopped
3. 1 cup fresh spinach, chopped
4. 1 red bell pepper, seeded and chopped
5. 2 scallions, chopped
6. ½ jalapeño pepper, seeded and chopped finely
7. Sea salt and freshly ground black pepper, to taste
8. 12 egg whites, beaten

Preparation of Bacon & Veggie Muffins

1. Preheat the oven to 350 degrees F.
2. In a large bowl, mix together bacon, vegetables, salt and black pepper.

3. Divide the vegetable mixture into 12 nonstick muffin cups

4. Pour egg whites over vegetables evenly.

5. Bake for 20 to 25 minutes or till egg whites are cooked through.

Calorie Count: Calories are 84 per serving

phase 2 lunch recipes

Philip Pablo

MEAL 17- GREEN GARDEN SALAD

Introduction

A refreshing, light yet satisfying and beautiful looking salad… This green salad is chock full of the flavors of fresh garden vegetables.

Preparation Time: 20 minutes

Cooking Time: 3 minutes

Serves: 6

Ingredients

For Salad

1. 1 cup green beans, sliced into 2-inch pieces

2. 1 cup green bell pepper, seeded and sliced thinly

Painless Fast Metabolism Diet Recipes for Lazy People

3. 1 cup cucumber, chopped

4. ½ cup scallion (green part), chopped

5. 2 cups lettuce leaves, torn

6. 2 tablespoons fresh cilantro, chopped

For Vinaigrette

1. 2 tablespoons cider vinegar

2. 1 garlic clove, minced

3. 1 teaspoon fresh green chili, seeded and minced

4. Sea salt and freshly ground black pepper, to taste

Preparation of Green Garden Salad

1. In a pan of boiling water, add beans and cook for about 3 minutes. Drain well.

2. Add all salad ingredients in a large bowl and mix.

3. Add vinaigrette ingredients in a small bowl and beat till well combined.

4. Pour vinaigrette on top of vegetable salad and toss to coat well.

5. Cover and refrigerate to chill before serving.

Calorie Count: Calories are 20 per serving

Philip Pablo

MEAL 18- Mushroom & Spinach Soup

Introduction

Delicious and elegant soup with healthy spinach and mushrooms. It is a great choice for soup lovers.

Preparation Time: 15 minutes

Cooking Time: 30 minutes

Serves: 4

Ingredients

1. 4 cups plus 2 tablespoons homemade chicken broth

Painless Fast Metabolism Diet Recipes for Lazy People

2. 1 cup shiitake mushrooms, sliced thinly

3. Sea salt, to taste

4. 8-10 garlic cloves, sliced thinly

5. ¼ cup apple cider vinegar

6. 1½ cups fresh spinach, torn

7. Freshly ground black pepper, to taste

Preparation of Mushroom & Spinach Soup

1. In a large nonstick soup pan, add 2 tablespoons of broth.

2. Add mushrooms and sprinkle with pinch of salt. Sauté for about 3 to 4 minutes.

3. Add garlic and sauté for 1 minute more.

4. Stir in vinegar and cook for 2 minutes.

5. Add spinach and cook for about 3 minutes.

6. Add remaining broth and bring to a boil.

7. Reduce the heat to low. Cover and simmer for about 15 to 20 minutes.

8. Stir in salt and black pepper and serve hot.

Calorie Count: Calories are 74 per serving

Philip Pablo

MEAL 19- PAN FRIED CHICKEN BREASTS

Introduction

A moist, tender, and delicious chicken dish. This recipe provides a very quick, and healthy way of cooking chicken.

Preparation Time: 20 minutes

Cooking Time: 16 minutes

Serves: 2

Ingredients

1. 1 tablespoon fresh rosemary, minced

Painless Fast Metabolism Diet Recipes for Lazy People

2. 1 garlic clove, minced
3. 3 teaspoons fresh lemon juice
4. 1¼ cups homemade chicken broth
5. ¼ teaspoon onion salt
6. ¼ teaspoon red pepper flakes
7. Sea salt and black pepper, to taste
8. 2 (4-ounce) skinless, boneless organic chicken breasts

Preparation of Pan Fried Chicken Breasts

1. In a large bowl, add all ingredients except chicken and mix well.
2. Add chicken and coat with mixture evenly.
3. Cover and refrigerate for at least 2 hours.
4. Heat a nonstick skillet on medium heat.
5. Add chicken and marinade to the skillet.
6. Cook for 3 minutes per side or till cooked through.
7. Transfer chicken onto a plate.
8. Cook the remaining marinade for about 3 to 4 minutes.
9. Return the chicken to the skillet.
10. Reduce the heat to low. Simmer for about 6 minutes, flipping once after 3 minutes.

Philip Pablo

Calorie Count: Calories are 176 per serving

MEAL 20- BROILED BEEF WITH BROCCOLI

Introduction

A great tasty dish for the whole family... Feed your family with this quick and healthy dish -- they will love it.

Preparation Time: 10 minutes

Cooking Time: 15 minutes

Serves: 2

Philip Pablo

Ingredients

1. 2 garlic cloves, minced

2. 1 tablespoon fresh lime juice

3. 1/8 teaspoon ground mustard

4. ¼ teaspoon dried rosemary, crushed

5. Sea salt and freshly ground black pepper, to taste

6. 2 (4-ounce) sirloin steaks

7. 2 cups broccoli florets

Preparation of Broiled Beef with Broccoli

1. Preheat the broiler. Place the rack 4-inches from heat element.

2. In a large bowl, add garlic, lime juice, mustard and spices.

3. Add steaks and coat with garlic mixture generously.

4. Broil for about 7 minutes.

5. Flip the steaks and broil for 7 to 8 minutes more.

6. Meanwhile put a steamer basket in a pan of boiling water on medium heat.

7. Place broccoli in steamer basket. Cover and cook for 4 to 5 minutes.

8. On a serving plate, place steak alongside broccoli and serve.

Calorie Count: Calories are 253 per serving

Painless Fast Metabolism Diet Recipes for Lazy People

phase 2 dinner recipes

Philip Pablo

MEAL 21- BEEF & VEGGIE SALAD

Introduction

A big hit recipe for a healthy salad. Welcome your family and friends to the dinner table with this healthy and delicious salad.

Preparation Time: 20 minutes

Cooking Time: 12 minutes

Serves: 4

Ingredients

1. 3 (4-ounce) organic skirt steaks, trimmed

2. 2 teaspoons garlic, minced

Painless Fast Metabolism Diet Recipes for Lazy People

3. Sea salt and freshly ground black pepper, to taste

4. 1 cup cucumber, chopped

5. 1 cup radish, sliced thinly

6. ½ cup yellow bell pepper, seeded and sliced thinly

7. ½ cup red bell pepper, seeded and sliced thinly

8. 1 cup scallion, chopped

9. 3 cups fresh spinach, chopped

10. 3 tablespoons fresh lemon juice

Preparation of Beef & Veggie Salad

1. Preheat the broiler. Place the rack 4-inches from heating element.

2. Rub the steaks evenly with minced garlic. Sprinkle with salt and black pepper generously.

3. Broil for about 5 to 7 minutes.

4. Flip the steaks and broil for 4 to 5 minutes more.

5. Remove from oven and put aside for 10 minutes before slicing. Cut into bite size pieces.

6. Meanwhile in a large serving bowl, mix together vegetables.

7. Sprinkle with salt and black pepper and drizzle with lemon juice.

8. Toss to coat well. Top with beef and serve.

Calorie Count: Calories are 208 per serving

Philip Pablo

MEAL 22- HOT BEEF & CABBAGE SOUP

Introduction

There is nothing better than this soup during the cold winter months. Even picky eaters will love this wonderfully delicious soup.

Preparation Time: 20 minutes

Cooking Time: 1 hour 25 minutes

Serves: 8

Ingredients

1. 2 tablespoons water

2. ½ cup onion, chopped

Painless Fast Metabolism Diet Recipes for Lazy People

3. 2 teaspoons garlic, minced

4. 2 pounds organic stew beef, trimmed

5. ½ cup fresh cilantro, chopped

6. ½ cup green chiles, chopped

7. ½ teaspoon ground cumin

8. ¼ teaspoon chili powder

9. ½ teaspoon red pepper flakes, crushed

10. Black pepper, to taste

11. 8 cups water

12. 8 cups homemade beef broth

13. 12 cups cabbage, shredded

14. ¼ cup fresh lime juice

15. Sea salt, to taste

Preparation of Hot Beef & Cabbage Soup

1. In a large nonstick soup pan, add 2 tablespoons of water.

2. Add onion and sauté for about 4 minutes.

3. Add garlic and sauté for 1 minute more.

4. Add beef, scallion, chiles and spices and cook for 4 to 5 minutes.

5. Add water and broth and bring to a boil on high heat.

6. Reduce the heat to medium. Stir in cabbage.

7. Cover and cook for 1 hour and 15 minutes.

8. Stir in lime juice and salt and remove from heat. Serve hot.

Calorie Count: Calories are 322 per serving

MEAL 23- ROASTED LAMB LEG WITH ROSEMARY

Introduction

A big hit for large gatherings or special occasions. This delicious main dish recipe uses garlic, fresh herbs and lemon juice to flavor the meat.

Preparation Time: 15 minutes

Cooking Time: 1 hour and 20 minutes

Serves: 8

Ingredients

1. 3 garlic cloves, crushed

2. 3 tablespoons fresh rosemary, chopped

3. 2 tablespoons fresh mint leaves, chopped

4. 1/3 cup fresh lemon juice

5. ½ teaspoon red pepper flakes, crushed

6. Sea salt and freshly ground black pepper, to taste

7. 1 (4 pound) butterflied lamb leg, trimmed

Preparation of Roasted Lamb Leg with Rosemary

1. In a small bowl mix together all ingredients except lamb leg. Keep aside.

2. With a sharp knife, make deep cuts all over lamb leg.

3. Place lamb in a large nonstick baking dish.

4. Coat the lamb leg with garlic mixture generously.

5. Roll the lamb and tie with kitchen string.

6. Put aside for at least 1 hour.

7. Preheat the oven to 450 degrees F. Place the rack in the middle of oven.

8. Roast for about 1 hour and 20 minutes.

9. Remove from oven and put aside for 10 to 15 minutes before slicing.

10. Remove kitchen strings and slice as desired, and serve.

Calorie Count: Calories are 155 per serving

Philip Pablo

MEAL 24- BAKED LEMONY FISH

Introduction

A wonderfully easy recipe with delicious results. Lemon slices bring a refreshingly tangy touch to fish fillets.

Preparation Time: 15 minutes

Cooking Time: 30 minutes

Serves: 4

Ingredients

1. 2 lemons, sliced thinly and divided

2. 4 shallots, sliced thinly and divided

Painless Fast Metabolism Diet Recipes for Lazy People

3. 4 (6-ounce) cod fillets

4. ¼ cup fresh rosemary, minced

5. ¼ teaspoon ground cumin

6. ¼ teaspoon cayenne pepper

7. Sea salt and black pepper, to taste

Preparation of Baked Lemony Fish

1. Preheat the oven to 450 degrees F.

2. Place half of lemon slices and shallots in a ceramic baking dish.

3. Sprinkle fish with rosemary and spices generously. Arrange fish fillets over lemon slices and shallots.

4. Spread remaining lemon slices and shallots over fish.

5. Bake for about 25 to 30 minutes.

Calorie Count: Calories are 165 per serving

Philip Pablo

phase 2 snacks recipes

Painless Fast Metabolism Diet Recipes for Lazy People

MEAL 25- BAKED MEATBALLS WITH VEGETABLES

Philip Pablo

Introduction

A wonderfully delicious twist on simple traditional meatballs... Mushrooms and spinach combines nicely with beef.

Preparation Time: 15 minutes

Cooking Time: 20 minutes

Serves: 6

Ingredients

1. 1½ pounds lean organic ground beef
2. ½ cup fresh mushrooms, chopped finely
3. 1½ cups fresh spinach, chopped finely
4. 4 scallions, chopped
5. ¼ cup fresh cilantro leaves, chopped
6. 3 garlic cloves, mined
7. 1 teaspoon dried thyme, crushed
8. ¼ teaspoon red pepper flakes, crushed
9. Sea salt and freshly ground black pepper, to taste

Preparation of Baked Meatballs with Vegetables

1. Preheat the oven to 375 degrees F. Line a baking sheet with parchment paper.

Painless Fast Metabolism Diet Recipes for Lazy People

2. In a large bowl, add all ingredients and mix till well combined.

3. Make desired sized meatballs from mixture.

4. Arrange balls on prepared baking sheet in a single layer.

5. Bake for about 20 minutes.

Calorie Count: Calories are 209 per serving

Philip Pablo

MEAL 26- Chicken & Bell Pepper Wraps

Introduction

A tantalizingly delicious wrap recipe. These chicken and bell pepper lettuce wraps are really light and full of flavor.

Preparation Time: 15 minutes

Serves: 2

Ingredients

1. 1 cup grilled chicken, sliced
2. ¼ cup seeded green bell pepper, thinly sliced

Painless Fast Metabolism Diet Recipes for Lazy People

3. ¼ cup seeded green bell pepper, thinly sliced

4. ¼ cup scallion, chopped

5. ¼ cup thinly sliced red onion

6. ¼ cup fresh basil leaves, minced

7. 1 teaspoon balsamic vinegar

8. Sea salt and freshly ground black pepper, to taste

9. 2 large fresh lettuce leaves

Preparation of Chicken & Bell Pepper Wraps

1. In a large bowl, mix together all ingredients except lettuce.

2. Divide the chicken mixture evenly on lettuce leaves.

3. Roll the leaves and serve.

Calorie Count: Calories are 143 per serving

Philip Pablo

phase 2 desserts recipes

MEAL 27- CITRUS SORBET

Introduction

One of the most refreshing and light desserts. This tart sorbet has a powerful citrus flavor.

Preparation Time: 15 minutes

Serves: 6

Ingredients

1. 1½ cups fresh lime juice

2. ½ cup fresh lemon juice

3. 2 cups water

4. 1 teaspoon liquid stevia

5. 1 tablespoon lemon zest, freshly grated

6. 1 tablespoon fresh mint leaves

Preparation of Citrus Sorbet

1. In a large bowl, add all ingredients and mix till well combined.

2. Cover and refrigerate for about 1 hour.

3. Transfer the mixture into an ice cream maker.

4. Process according to manufacturer's directions.

5. Transfer the sorbet into a container. Cover and freeze for at least 4 to 5 hours.

6. Garnish with mint leaves and serve.

Calorie Count: Calories are 20 per serving

MEAL 28- GREEN POPSICLES

Introduction

A great combo of the freshest summer flavors. These light and refreshing cucumber and mint popsicles are a great hit during the blazing hot summer days.

Preparation Time: 10 minutes

Cooking Time: 2 minutes

Serves: 4

Ingredients

1. ½ cup water

Philip Pablo

2. 1 cup fresh mint leaves

3. 1 teaspoon lime zest, freshly grated

4. 1 cucumber, peeled, seeded and sliced

5. 1/3 cup fresh lime juice

6. 1 teaspoon liquid stevia

Preparation of Green Popsicles

1. In a small pan, add water, mint leaves and lime zest. Bring to a boil on medium heat.

2. Remove from heat and strain the mint and lime zest. Let it cool slightly.

3. In a food processor, add cucumber and pulse till chopped very finely.

4. Add mint syrup and remaining ingredients and pulse till smooth.

5. Transfer the mixture into Popsicle molds.

6. Freeze to set completely.

Calorie Count: Calories are 27 per serving

phase 3 breakfast recipes

Philip Pablo

MEAL 29- BACON & VEGETABLE FRITTATA

Introduction

A versatile recipe for breakfast. Bacon with eggs and fresh vegetables makes this frittata hearty and delicious.

Preparation Time: 15 minutes

Cooking Time: 25 minutes

Serves: 6

Ingredients

1. 6 large eggs

Painless Fast Metabolism Diet Recipes for Lazy People

2. 2 teaspoons garlic powder

3. ¼ teaspoon red pepper flakes, crushed

4. Sea salt and freshly ground black pepper, to taste

5. 1 tablespoon olive oil

6. 4 strips nitrate-free turkey bacon, chopped

7. 1 cup fresh spinach, chopped

8. 1 cup fresh mushrooms, chopped

9. ¾ cup grape tomatoes, chopped

10.

Preparation of Bacon & Vegetable Frittata

1. Preheat the oven to 350 degrees F.

2. In a bowl, add eggs and seasoning and beat till well combined.

3. Add oil to an oven proof skillet and heat on medium heat.

4. Add bacon, spinach, mushrooms and tomatoes and sauté for about 2 minutes.

5. Pour egg mixture on top. Cook for about 2 to 3 minutes.

6. Now, transfer the skillet to preheated oven. Bake in oven for about 15 to 20 minutes or till

eggs are done completely.

Calorie Count: Calories are 170 per serving

Philip Pablo

MEAL 30- BREAD WITH HAZELNUT BUTTER AND BERRIES

Introduction

A super-fast and easy breakfast with healthy nutrients… Fresh berries give a wonderful flavor to buttered slices.

Preparation Time: 5 minutes

Serves: 2

Ingredients

1. 2 sprouted grain bread slices, toasted

2. ¼ cup unsweetened hazelnut butter

3. ½ cup fresh raspberries

4. ½ cup fresh blackberries

5. 1/8 teaspoon ground cinnamon

Preparation of Bread with Hazelnut Butter and Berries

1. Spread the hazelnut butter on both slices evenly.

2. Place berries on top.

3. Sprinkle with cinnamon and serve.

Calorie Count: Calories are 290 per serving

Painless Fast Metabolism Diet Recipes for Lazy People

MEAL 31- LEMONY BLUEBERRY PANCAKES

Introduction

These delicious quinoa pancakes are really sweet, moist and fluffy. These pancakes are sure to become your kid's favorite breakfast.

Preparation Time: 15 minutes

Cooking Time: 4 minutes

Serves: 2

Ingredients

1. 1 cup cooked quinoa

Philip Pablo

2. 1 teaspoon baking soda

3. Pinch of sea salt

4. 1½ tablespoons grape seed oil, divided

5. 2 eggs

6. ¼ cup unsweetened almond milk

7. 10-12 drops liquid stevia

8. 1 tablespoon fresh lemon juice

9. 1 teaspoon lime zest, freshly grated

10. 1 cup fresh blueberries, divided

Preparation of Lemony Blueberry Pancakes

1. In a large blender, add quinoa, baking soda, and salt, and pulse till well combined.

2. Add 1 tablespoon of oil and remaining ingredients except blueberries and pulse till smooth.

3. Transfer the mixture into a large bowl. Fold in ½ cup of blueberries.

4. In a large skillet, heat remaining oil on medium heat.

5. Add ¼ cup of mixture in skillet. Cook for about 4 minutes, flipping once after 2 minutes.

6. Repeat with the remaining mixture.

7. Top with remaining blueberries and serve.

Painless Fast Metabolism Diet Recipes for Lazy People

Calorie Count: Calories are 225 per serving

Philip Pablo

MEAL 32- OATS WITH ALMOND BUTTER & CHERRIES

Introduction

This thick, chewy and delicious breakfast is loaded with energy-delivering ingreadients. Cherries add a natural sweetness to the oats.

Preparation Time: 10 minutes, plus 8 hours soaking time

Cooking Time: 11 minutes

Serves: 8

Ingredients

1. 4 cups water

2. 1 cup steel-cut oats

3. ¼ cup almond butter

4. 1 cup dark red cherries

Preparation of Oats with Almond Butter & Cherries

1. In a large pan, add water and oats on medium heat.

2. Bring to a boil for about 1 minute. Cover the pan and remove from heat.

3. Put aside overnight.

4. In the morning, uncover the pan and place on medium heat.

5. Bring to a boil. Reduce the heat to low. Simmer, stirring occasionally for about 8 to 10 minutes.

6. Remove from heat and immediately stir in almond butter.

7. Top with cherries and serve.

Calorie Count: Calories are 143 per serving

Philip Pablo

phase 3 lunch recipes

MEAL 33- Pasta & Veggie Salad with Creamy Dressing

Introduction

An incredible salad which is creamy, a little tangy and crunchy… your whole family will love it.

Preparation Time: 20 minutes

Serves: 4

Ingredients

For Salad:

Philip Pablo

1. 2 cups cooked quinoa fusilli pasta
2. 1 yellow bell pepper, seeded and sliced
3. ½ cup black olives, pitted and sliced
4. 1 cucumber, chopped
5. 1½ cups fresh cherry tomatoes, halved
6. 1 red onion, sliced

For Creamy Dressing:

1. ½ cup mayonnaise (safflower)
2. 2 tablespoons balsamic vinegar
3. 1 tablespoon olive oil
4. 1 teaspoon Dijon mustard
5. 1 garlic clove, minced finely
6. ¼ teaspoon fresh basil, minced
7. Sea salt and black pepper, to taste

Preparation of Pasta & Veggie Salad with Creamy Dressing

1. Add all salad ingredients in a large bowl and mix.

2. In another bowl, add all dressing ingredients and mix till well combined.

3. Pour dressing over salad and gently, mix to combine.

4. Serve immediately.

Calorie Count: Calories are 290 per serving

Philip Pablo

MEAL 34- Veggie soup with Quinoa

Introduction

A vegetarian soup which is delicious and healthy … It is loaded with healthy nutrients and will surely warm your soul.

Preparation Time: 20 minutes

Cooking Time: 40 minutes

Serves: 8

Ingredients

1. 2 tablespoons coconut oil

Painless Fast Metabolism Diet Recipes for Lazy People

2. 1 medium white onion, chopped

3. 2 garlic cloves, minced

4. 2 yellow squash, peeled and chopped

5. 2 medium carrots, peeled and chopped

6. 1 ½ cups fresh green beans, sliced into ½-inch pieces

7. 2 stalks celery, chopped

8. 1 (14-ounce) can diced tomatoes

9. ¼ cup plus fresh parsley, chopped with liquid

10. 4 cups homemade vegetable broth

11. 2 bay leaves

12. 2 cups cooked quinoa

13. Sea salt and freshly ground black pepper, to taste

14. 2 tablespoons fresh scallion (green part)

15. 2 tablespoons fresh parsley leaves, chopped

Preparation of Veggie soup with Quinoa

1. Heat oil in a large pan on medium heat.

2. Add onion and sauté for about 4 to 5 minutes.

3. Add garlic and sauté for 1 minute more.

4. Add fresh vegetables and cook, stirring often for 3 to 4 minutes.

5. Add tomatoes, parsley and broth. Bring to a boil on medium-high heat.

6. Reduce the heat to low. Simmer, covered for about 25 to 30 minutes.

7. Stir in quinoa, salt and pepper and remove from heat.

8. Top with scallion and parsley leaves and serve hot.

Calorie Count: Calories are 234 per serving

Painless Fast Metabolism Diet Recipes for Lazy People

MEAL 35- BAKED ROSEMARY CHICKEN & TOMATOES

Philip Pablo

Introduction

The combo of rosemary with chicken and cherry tomatoes is a hit. Rosemary gives a wonderful flavor to this dish.

Preparation Time: 15 minutes

Cooking Time: 1 hour minutes

Serves: 6

Ingredients

1. 6 (4-ounce) skinless, boneless chicken thighs

2. 2 cups cherry tomatoes

3. ½ cup fresh rosemary

4. 1 tablespoon olive oil

5. ½ teaspoon garlic powder

6. ½ teaspoon red pepper flakes, crushed

7. Sea salt and freshly ground black pepper, to taste

Preparation of Baked Rosemary Chicken & Tomatoes

1. Preheat the oven to 425 degrees F. Line a large baking dish with parchment paper.

2. Place chicken thighs on prepared baking dish in a single layer.

3. Spread tomatoes and rosemary over chicken.

4. Drizzle with oil evenly.

Painless Fast Metabolism Diet Recipes for Lazy People

5. Sprinkle with garlic powder, red pepper flakes, salt and black pepper.

6. Bake for about 45 to 55 minutes.

Calorie Count: Calories are 187 per serving

Philip Pablo

MEAL 36- Shrimp with Mushrooms

Introduction

A super quick and easy dish for lunch. This combination of shrimp and mushrooms is delicious, and succulent.

Preparation Time: 10 minutes

Cooking Time: 17 minutes

Serves: 4

Ingredients

1. 1 tablespoon olive oil

2. ¼ cup onion, chopped

Painless Fast Metabolism Diet Recipes for Lazy People

3. 2 garlic cloves, minced

4. 1 cup fresh mushrooms, sliced

5. 2 pounds shrimp, peeled and deveined

6. Sea salt and freshly ground black pepper, to taste

7. ¼ cup chicken broth

8. 2 tablespoons scallions (green part), chopped

Preparation of Shrimp with Mushrooms

1. In a large skillet, heat oil on medium heat.

2. Add onion and sauté for 4 to 5 minutes.

3. Add garlic and sauté for 1 minute.

4. Add mushrooms and cook for 4 to 5 minutes.

5. Add shrimp and season with salt and black pepper.

6. Cook for 2 to 3 minutes.

7. Add broth and cook for 2 to 3 minutes more.

8. Stir in scallions and serve hot.

Calorie Count: Calories are 312 per serving

Philip Pablo

MEAL 37- GRILLED TANGY VEGETABLES

Introduction

These marinated and grilled vegetables are a versatile and easy dish, perfect for vegetables in season. This marinade adds a wonderful flavoring to vegetables.

Preparation Time: 20 minutes

Cooking Time: 10 minutes

Serves: 6

Ingredients

1. 1 large yellow squash, sliced thinly (½-inch pieces)

Painless Fast Metabolism Diet Recipes for Lazy People

2. 1 large zucchini, sliced thinly (½-inch pieces)

3. 1 medium eggplant, sliced thinly (½-inch pieces)

4. 2 tomatoes, sliced into 4 pieces

5. ¼ cup olive oil

6. 2 tablespoons balsamic vinegar

7. 2 tablespoons fresh lemon juice

8. 2 garlic cloves, minced

9. ¼ cup fresh oregano, minced

10. ¼ cup fresh thyme, minced

11. ¼ teaspoon red pepper flakes, crushed

12. Sea salt, to taste

13. Black pepper, to taste

Preparation of Grilled Tangy Vegetables

1. Preheat your grill to medium-high heat. Lightly grease the grill grate.

2. In a large bowl, add all vegetables.

3. In another small bowl, add remaining ingredients and mix till well combined. Put aside for 5

minutes.

4. Add oil mixture to bowl of vegetables. Toss to coat well.

5. Arrange the vegetables on heated grill. Cook for 4 to 5 on each side.

Philip Pablo

Calorie Count: Calories are 195 per serving

phase 3 dinner recipes

Philip Pablo

MEAL 38- Spiced Chickpeas & Sweet Potato Salad

Introduction

A colorful and healthy, but delicious salad for a buffet at a family gathering. The spices are a nice combination with the sweet potato and chickpeas.

Preparation Time: 20 minutes

Cooking Time: 17 minutes

Serves: 6

Painless Fast Metabolism Diet Recipes for Lazy People

Ingredients

1. 1 medium sweet potato, peeled and cubed

2. 2 tablespoons olive oil, divided

3. Sea salt and black pepper, to taste

4. 2 teaspoons ground cumin, divided

5. 1 teaspoon ground coriander

6. 1 (16-ounce) can chickpeas, drained

7. 1 small red onion, chopped

8. 1 cucumber, chopped

9. ½ cup chopped fresh parsley

10. 1 tablespoon fresh lemon juice

11. 1 teaspoon lemon zest, freshly grated

12. 1 teaspoon ground coriander

13. ½ teaspoon red pepper flakes, crushed

14.

Preparation of Spiced Chickpeas & Sweet Potato Salad

1. In a pan of boiling water, add sweet potato and cook for 10 to 12 minutes. Drain well.

2. In a skillet, heat 1 tablespoon of oil on medium heat.

3. Add sweet potato and cook for about 4 to 5 minutes.

4. Add salt, black pepper, 1 teaspoon of cumin and coriander and cook for 1 to 2 minutes.

5. Remove from heat and cool slightly.

6. In a large serving bowl, add sweet potato, onion, cucumber, lemon juice, zest and spices and mix

well.

7. Drizzle with remaining oil and serve.

Calorie Count: Calories are 351 per serving

MEAL 39- CHICKEN, BARLEY & VEGGIE SOUP

Introduction

A perfect comfort food for a cold winter's night. This soup is really hearty and delicious with the flavors of chicken, barley and vegetables.

Preparation Time: 20 minutes

Cooking Time: 2 hours 40 minutes

Serves: 8

Ingredients

1. 1 tablespoon olive oil

Philip Pablo

2. 1 cup onion, diced

3. 1 tablespoon garlic, minced

4. 2 pounds skinless, boneless organic chicken breasts

5. 6 cups homemade chicken broth

6. 4 cups water

7. 1 cup white barley

8. 2 cups broccoli florets, chopped

9. 2 cups zucchini, cubed

10. 2 cups butternut squash, cubed

11. 1 cup fresh cilantro, chopped

12. Sea salt and freshly ground black pepper, to taste

13.

Preparation of Chicken, Barley & Veggie Soup

1. In a large soup pan, heat oil on medium heat.

2. Add onion and garlic and sauté for 4 to 5 minutes.

3. Add chicken and cook for about 4 to 5 minutes.

4. Add broth and water and boil for 5 minutes on high heat.

5. Now, turn down the heat to low. Cover and simmer for about 1 hour.

6. Transfer chicken onto a plate, cut chicken into small pieces.

7. Add barley, vegetables and cilantro and bring to a boil on high heat.

8. Reduce the heat to low. Cover and simmer for about 1 hour.

9. Return the chicken to the pan. Simmer, uncovered for 30 minutes more.

10. Season with salt and black pepper and serve hot.

Calorie Count: Calories are 303 per serving

Philip Pablo

MEAL 40- BEEF & GREEN CHILES STEW

Introduction

One of the best traditional holiday stews. This hearty and tasty stew will be a great hit for winter dinners.

Preparation Time: 20 minutes

Cooking Time: 40 minutes

Serves: 6

Ingredients

1. 3 tablespoons olive oil

Painless Fast Metabolism Diet Recipes for Lazy People

2. 1 large white onion, chopped

3. 3 garlic cloves, minced

4. 1½ pounds organic sirloin beef, trimmed and cubed

5. 2 large fresh tomatoes, chopped finely

6. 1 teaspoon dried oregano, crushed

7. 6 roasted green chiles, peeled and chopped

8. ½ head cabbage, chopped

9. 1 large sweet potato, peeled and cubed

10. 6 cups homemade beef broth

11. Sea salt and freshly ground black pepper, to taste

12. ½ cup fresh cilantro, minced

Preparation of Beef & Green Chiles Stew

1. In a large soup pan, heat oil on medium heat.

2. Add onion and sauté for 4 to 5 minutes.

3. Add garlic and sauté for 1 minute.

4. Add beef and cook for 4 to 5 minutes.

5. Add tomatoes and cook for 3 to 4 minutes.

6. Add remaining ingredients and bring to a boil.

7. Reduce the heat to low. Cover and simmer for about 1 hour.

Philip Pablo

Calorie Count: Calories are 373 per serving

MEAL 41- GRILLED LAMB CHOPS WITH TOMATO SALAD

Introduction

The Citrus mixture balances enhances the flavor of hot grilled lamb chops. Fresh tomato salad makes it a full meal.

Preparation Time: 20 minutes

Cooking Time: 40 minutes

Serves: 4

Ingredients

Philip Pablo

For Chops

1. 4 (4-ounce) organic lamb chops, trimmed
2. ¼ teaspoon red pepper flakes, crushed
3. Sea salt and freshly ground black pepper, taste

For Tomato Salad

1. 1 garlic clove, minced
2. 2 tablespoons fresh cilantro, minced
3. 2 tablespoons fresh lemon juice
4. 2 tablespoons olive oil
5. ¼ teaspoon red pepper flakes, crushed
6. Sea salt and freshly ground black pepper, to taste
7. 1 cup fresh tomatoes, sliced
8. 4 cups fresh mixed greens, torn

Preparation of Grilled lamb Chops with Tomato Salad

1. Preheat the grill to medium-high heat. Grease the grill grate.
2. Sprinkle the chops with salt and black pepper generously.
3. Cook the chops for about 6 minutes, flipping once after 3 minutes.
4. Meanwhile in small bowl, add garlic, cilantro, lemon juice, oil, red pepper flakes, salt and black pepper and mix well.
5. On a large serving plate, place greens.

Painless Fast Metabolism Diet Recipes for Lazy People

6. Place chops and tomatoes over greens. Drizzle with garlic mixture and serve.

Calorie Count: Calories are 400 per serving

Philip Pablo

MEAL 42- BEANS & VEGETABLES BAKE

Introduction

A classic and delightful main dish for the whole family… It has a great combination of beans and vegetables with a tasty topping.

Preparation Time: 20 minutes

Cooking Time: 1 hour 10 minutes

Serves: 8

Ingredients

1. 1 tablespoon olive oil

2. 2 large white onions, chopped

Painless Fast Metabolism Diet Recipes for Lazy People

3. 4 garlic cloves, minced

4. 1 small carrot, peeled and chopped

5. 1 red bell pepper, seeded and chopped

6. 1 stalk celery, chopped

7. 1 (15-ounce) can great northern beans, drained

8. 1 (15-ounce) can lima beans, drained

9. 1 (8-ounce) can sugar-free tomato sauce

10. 1 tablespoon Dijon mustard

11. 1 tablespoon cider vinegar

12. 2 teaspoons tamari

13. 1 teaspoon smoked paprika

14. ¼ teaspoon chili powder

15. Sea salt and freshly ground black pepper, taste

Preparation of Beans & Vegetables Bake

1. Preheat the oven to 350 degrees F. Grease a baking dish.

2. In a large skillet, heat oil on medium heat.

3. Add onion and sauté for about 4 to 5 minutes.

4. Add garlic and sauté for about 1 minute.

5. Add vegetables and cook for 3 to 4 minutes.

6. Stir in beans and immediately remove from heat.

7. Transfer the mixture to the prepared baking dish.

8. In a blender, add remaining ingredients and pulse till smooth.

9. Spread tomato sauce mixture over beans mixture evenly.

10. Cover and bake for about 30 minutes.

11. Remove the cover and bake for 30 minutes more.

Calorie Count: Calories are 293 per serving

Painless Fast Metabolism Diet Recipes for Lazy People

phase 3 snacks recipes

Philip Pablo

MEAL 43- S<small>PICY</small> S<small>WEET</small> P<small>OTATO</small> W<small>EDGES</small>

Introduction

An easy and perfect way to prepare a sweet potato as a snack…This easy and quick snack is really delicious.

Preparation Time: 15 minutes

Cooking Time: 20 minutes

Serves: 6

Painless Fast Metabolism Diet Recipes for Lazy People

Ingredients

1. 2 large sweet potatoes, peeled and cut into wedges

2. 2 tablespoons olive oil

3. ¼ teaspoon red pepper flakes, crushed

4. ½ teaspoon ground cumin

5. Sea salt, to taste

6. 2 tablespoons fresh cilantro, chopped

Preparation of Spicy Sweet Potato Wedges

1. Preheat the oven to 400 degrees F. Line a baking sheet with parchment paper.

2. Coat sweet potato wedges with 1 tablespoon of oil.

3. Arrange wedges on prepared baking sheet.

4. Bake for about 10 minutes. Remove from oven.

5. Meanwhile preheat the grill to medium-high heat. Grease the grill grate.

6. In a bowl, add baked sweet potato wedges, remaining oil and spices and toss to coat well.

7. Grill for 10 minutes, flipping once after 5 minutes.

8. Garnish with chopped cilantro before serving.

Philip Pablo

Calorie Count: Calories are 100 per serving

MEAL 44- HERBED CHICKPEA PATTIES

Introduction

A vegetarian snack which is healthy and tasty. These crunchy patties are really flavorful.

Preparation Time: 15 minutes

Cooking Time: 25 minutes

Serves: 5

Ingredients

1. 1 teaspoon coconut oil

2. 1 small onion, chopped

3. 1 clove garlic, finely minced

4. ½ teaspoon dried thyme, crushed

5. 19-ounce canned chickpeas, drained and mashed

6. 2 tablespoons fresh cilantro, chopped

7. 1 egg white

8. Sea salt and black pepper, as required

Preparation of Herbed Chickpeas Patties

1. Preheat the oven to 425 degrees F. Line a baking sheet with parchment paper.

2. In a skillet, heat oil on medium heat.

3. Sauté onion in heated oil for about 4 minutes.

4. Add garlic and sauté for 1 minute more.

5. Transfer the onion mixture into a bowl.

6. Add mashed chickpeas and remaining ingredients and mix till well combined.

7. Make 5 equal sized patties from mixture.

8. Arrange the patties on prepared baking sheet in a single layer.

9. Bake for 10 minutes. Flip patties over and bake for 10 minutes more.

Calorie Count: Calories are 410 per serving

MEAL 45- TANGY CABBAGE COLESLAW

Introduction

A simple and delightful coleslaw with wonderful flavors. This salad is perfectly tangy.

Preparation Time: 10 minutes

Serves: 4

Ingredients

1. 1 small green cabbage, shredded finely

2. 2 tablespoons apple cider vinegar

3. 1 tablespoon olive oil

Philip Pablo

4. ¼ teaspoon mustard powder

5. ¼ teaspoon celery seed

6. 1/8 teaspoon cumin seed

7. Sea salt and freshly ground black pepper, to taste

8.

Preparation of Tangy Cabbage Coleslaw

1. In a large bowl, place cabbage.

2. In another small bowl, add remaining ingredients and mix well.

3. Pour vinaigrette over cabbage and toss to coat well.

4. Cover and refrigerate to chill before serving.

Calorie Count: Calories are 78 per serving

Painless Fast Metabolism Diet Recipes for Lazy People

phase 3 desserts recipes

Philip Pablo

MEAL 46- NUTTY OATMEAL COOKIES

Introduction

Quick, easy and incredibly delicious and soft cookies... These oatmeal cookies get a sophisticated twist from the addition of tahini.

Preparation Time: 10 minutes

Cooking Time: 10 minutes

Serves: 6

Ingredients

1. 1/3 cup birch xylitol

2. 1 cup oatmeal

Painless Fast Metabolism Diet Recipes for Lazy People

3. ½ cup walnuts, chopped

4. 1 egg

5. ½ cup tahini

6. 1 cup unsweetened coconut, shredded

7. ½ teaspoon ground nutmeg

8. ½ teaspoon ground cinnamon

9. Pinch of sea salt

Preparation of Nutty Oatmeal Cookies

1. Preheat the oven to 350 degrees F. Grease a cookie sheet.

2. In a blender, add birch xylitol and pulse to a fine powder.

3. In a large bowl, add powdered xylitol and remaining ingredients and mix till well combined.

4. Drop spoonfuls of dough onto prepared cookie sheet in a single layer.

5. Bake for about 10 minutes.

Calorie Count: Calories are 303 per serving

Philip Pablo

MEAL 47- GRILLED PEACHES WITH GLAZE

Introduction

A sophisticated and simply delicious dessert. Balsamic glaze enhances the flavor of grilled peaches.

Preparation Time: 10 minutes

Cooking Time: 7 minutes

Serves: 6

Ingredients

1. 6 peaches, pitted and halved

2. ½ cup balsamic vinegar

3. ¼ teaspoon fresh ginger

4. Pinch of sea salt

5. ¼ teaspoon freshly ground black pepper

6. 22-25 drops liquid stevia

Preparation of Grilled Peaches with Glaze

1. Preheat grill to high heat. Grease the grill grate.

2. Place the peaches, cut side down on grill.

3. Grill for about 3 to 5 minutes. Transfer the peaches into a serving plate.

4. Meanwhile in a small pan, add vinegar, ginger, salt and black pepper on medium-high heat.

5. Cook for about 1 to 2 minutes. Discard the ginger.

6. Remove from heat and immediately, stir in stevia.

7. Pour vinegar glaze over peaches and serve.

Calorie Count: Calories are 43 per serving

Philip Pablo

MEAL 48-Rhubarb Compote

Introduction

One of the simplest and delicious ways of using fresh rhubarb. Lemon juice, vanilla and cinnamon add subtle flavors to this easy dessert.

Preparation Time: 15 minutes

Cooking Time: 10 minutes

Serves: 6

Ingredients

1. 1 cup birch xylitol

2. 4 cups fresh rhubarb, cut into ½-inch pieces

3. ¼ teaspoon ground cinnamon

4. 2 tablespoons fresh lemon juice

5. 1 teaspoon vanilla extract

6. 1/8 teaspoon cream of tartar

7. 2 large egg whites

Preparation of Rhubarb Compote

1. In a blender, add birch xylitol and pulse to a fine powder.

2. In a nonstick pan, add powdered xylitol, rhubarb, cinnamon and lemon juice on medium heat.

3. Cook, stirring continuously for 2 to 3 minutes.

4. Reduce the heat to medium-low. Cover and simmer, stirring occasionally for about 6 to 7

minutes.

5. Stir in vanilla and immediately remove from heat. Let it cool at room temperature.

6. In a small bowl, add cream of tartar and egg whites and beat till stiff peaks form.

7. Gently fold egg white mixture into rhubarb compote.

8. Transfer into serving bowls. Refrigerate to chill before serving.

Calorie Count: Calories are 53 per serving

Philip Pablo

MEAL 49- BLACKBERRY COBBLE

Introduction

A good dessert recipe to use fresh blackberries when in abundance in summer. This cobbler is filled with mouthwatering fresh blackberries.

Preparation Time: 10 minutes

Cooking Time: 35 minutes

Serves: 8

Ingredients

1. 3 cups fresh blackberries

2. 1½ cups almond flour

3. ½ teaspoon ground cinnamon

Painless Fast Metabolism Diet Recipes for Lazy People

4. Pinch of sea salt

5. 2 tablespoons coconut oil, melted

6. 1 egg

Preparation of Blackberry Cobbler

1. Preheat the oven to 350 degrees F. Lightly grease a pie pan.

2. Place blackberries in prepared pie pan.

3. In a bowl, mix together flour, cinnamon and salt.

4. In another bowl, add oil and egg and beat till well combined.

5. Mix egg mixture and flour mixture with a fork till crumbly.

6. Spread flour mixture over blackberries evenly.

7. Bake for about 35 minutes

Calorie Count: Calories are 91 per serving

Philip Pablo

MEAL 50- Avocado &Mint Mousse

Introduction

A delicious creamy dessert that incorporates fruit, healthy fat, and protein! This dessert is sure tosatisfy your sweet tooth.

Preparation Time: 5 minutes

Serves: 6

Ingredients

1. 2 ripe avocados, peeled, pitted and sliced

2. 1 teaspoon fresh mint leaves, chopped

3. 1¾ cups canned unsweetened coconut milk

4. ¼ cup coconut oil

5. 2 drops liquid stevia

6. 1 teaspoon vanilla extract

Preparation of Avocado & Mint Mousse

1. In a food processor, add all ingredients and pulse till smooth.

2. Transfer into serving bowls.

3. Refrigerate to chill for 10 to 15 minutes before serving.

Calorie Count: Calories are 362 per serving

Philip Pablo

BOOKS BY PHILLIP PABLO:

Painless Paleo Cooking For Lazy People

Kindle book link: http://www.amazon.com/dp/B00JG6Y9Z6

Paperback link: http://www.amazon.com/dp/1497530105

Audible link: http://www.amazon.com/dp/B00L2N7Y12

Painless Paleo Slow Cooker Recipes For Lazy People

Kindle book link: http://www.amazon.com/dp/B00JLYEYTE

Paperback link: http://www.amazon.com/dp/1499100744

Audible link: http://www.amazon.com/dp/B00L83GNSG

Painless Fast Metabolism Diet Recipes for Lazy People

Surprisingly Simple Smoothies Recipes For Lazy People

Kindle book link: http://www.amazon.com/dp/B00JTFOTUY

Paperback link: http://www.amazon.com/dp/149919739X

Audible link: http://www.amazon.com/dp/B00KQ1ZRZG

Painless Sugar Detox Recipes for Lazy People

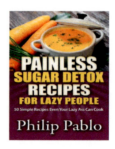

Kindle book link: http://www.amazon.com/dp/B00KEB81F6

Paperback link: http://www.amazon.com/dp/1499590105

Audible link: http://www.amazon.com/dp/B00M3DQ7MW

Philip Pablo

Painless Whole Food Recipes For Lazy People

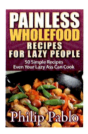

Kindle book link: http://www.amazon.com/dp/B00KESNLNQ

Paperback link: http://www.amazon.com/dp/1499591535

Audible link: http://www.amazon.com/dp/B00M8E6BCM

Surprisingly Simple Super Shred Diet Recipes For Lazy People

Kindle book link: http://www.amazon.com/dp/B00KH79CUK

Paperback link: http://www.amazon.com/dp/1499624603

Audible link: http://www.amazon.com/dp/B00N5AFAI4

Painless Fast Metabolism Diet Recipes for Lazy People

SURPRISINGLY SIMPLE COMFORT FOOD RECIPES FOR LAZY PEOPLE

Kindle book link: http://www.amazon.com/dp/B00LAAGR88

Paperback link: http://www.amazon.com/dp/1500283347

Surprisingly Simple Grains Free Recipes For Lazy People

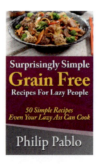

Kindle book link: http://www.amazon.com/dp/B00L5MV196

Paperback link: http://www.amazon.com/dp/150020837X

Philip Pablo

Surprisingly Simple Coconut Oil Recipes For Lazy People

Kindle book link: http://www.amazon.com/dp/B00L5MV1BO

Paperback link: http://www.amazon.com/dp/150020871X

Surprisingly Simple Super Shred Diet Recipes For Lazy People

Kindle book link: http://www.amazon.com/dp/B00KH79CUK

Paperback link: http://www.amazon.com/dp/1499624603

Audible link: http://www.amazon.com/dp/B00N5AFAI4

Painless Fast Metabolism Diet Recipes for Lazy People

Painless Mediterranean Diet Recipes For Lazy People

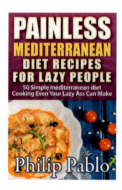

Kindle book link: http://www.amazon.com/dp/B00M0DYFSS

Paperback link: http://www.amazon.com/dp/1500587753

Painless Vegan Slow Cooker Recipes For Lazy People

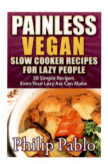

Kindle book link: http://www.amazon.com/dp/B00M0SRKBW

Paperback link: http://www.amazon.com/dp/1500588032

Philip Pablo

Painless Dash Diet Recipes For Lazy People

Kindle book link: http://www.amazon.com/dp/B00MMYSZHC

Paperback link: http://www.amazon.com/dp/1500798517

Audiobook link: http://www.amazon.com/dp/B00ODI51KE

Painless Ketogenic Diet Recipes For Lazy People

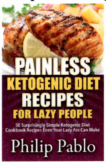

Kindle book link: http://www.amazon.com/dp/B00NLS9612

Paperback link: http://www.amazon.com/dp/1502376350

Painless Fast Metabolism Diet Recipes for Lazy People

Painless Leptin Diet Recipes For Lazy People

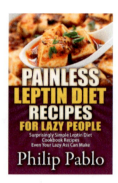

Kindle book link: http://www.amazon.com/dp/B00NG86E76

Paperback link: http://www.amazon.com/dp/1502301202

Philip Pablo

Recommended readings

1. The Fast Metabolism Diet: Eat More Food and Lose More Weight

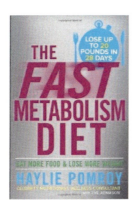

2. The Fast Metabolism Diet Cookbook: Eat Even More Food and Lose Even More Weight

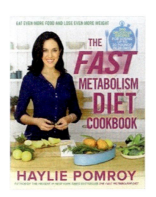

Painless Fast Metabolism Diet Recipes for Lazy People

ABOUT THE AUTHOR

Phillip Pablo is a professional chef with a lot of unique recipes. He is also an editor with a local food magazine and understands cooking and the importance of having accurate recipes.

Made in the USA
Middletown, DE
31 July 2018